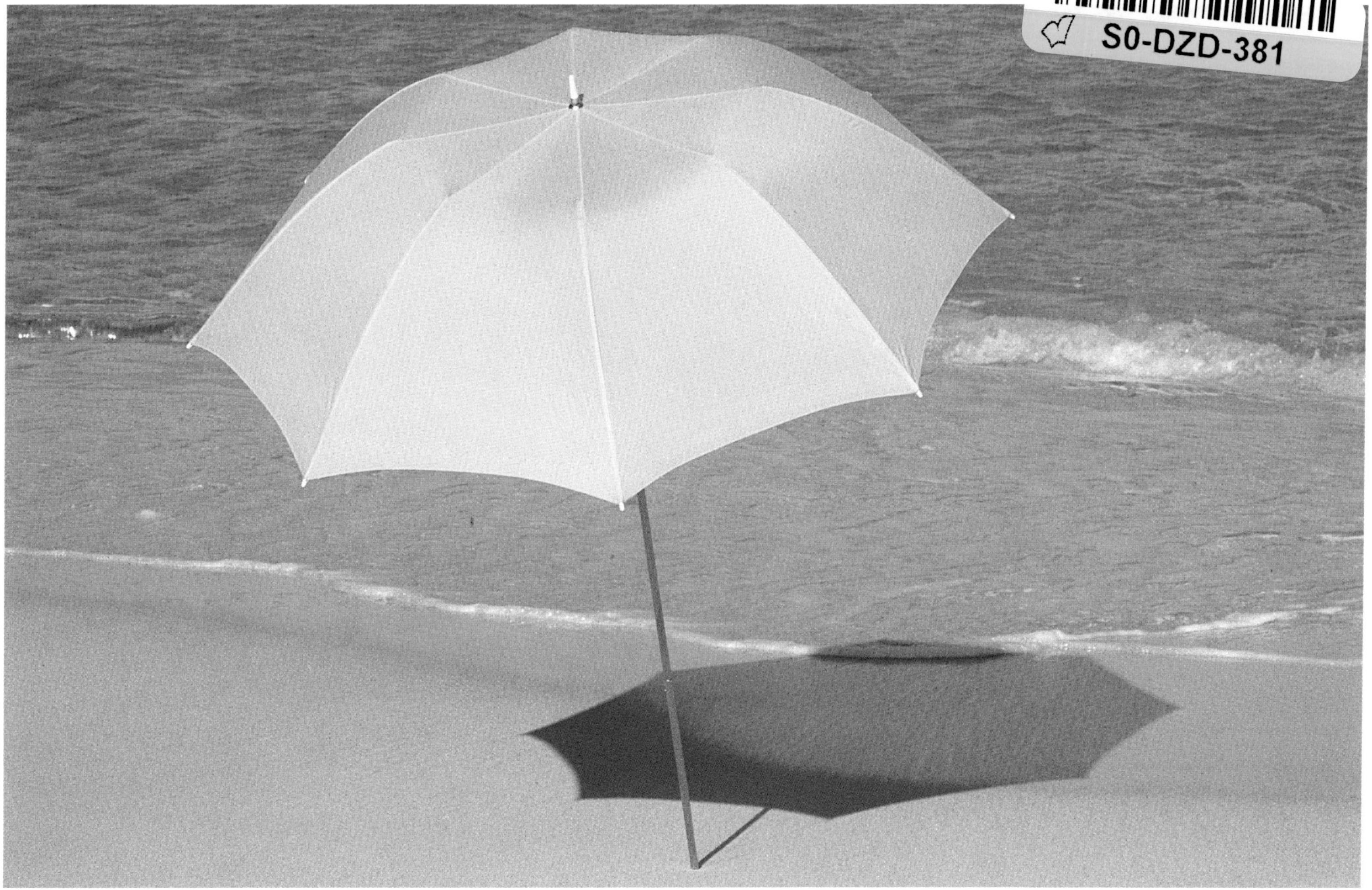

umbrella

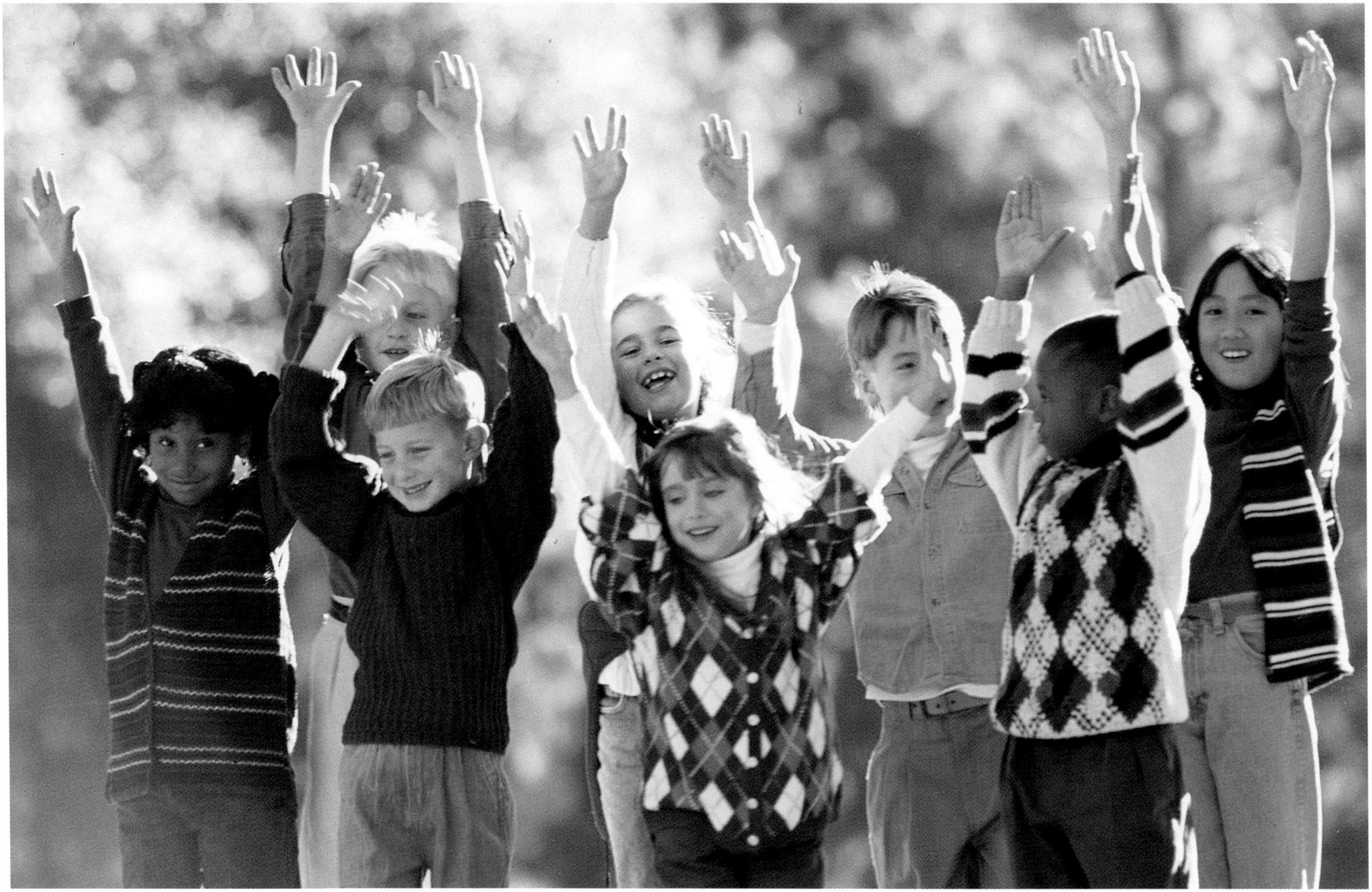

up

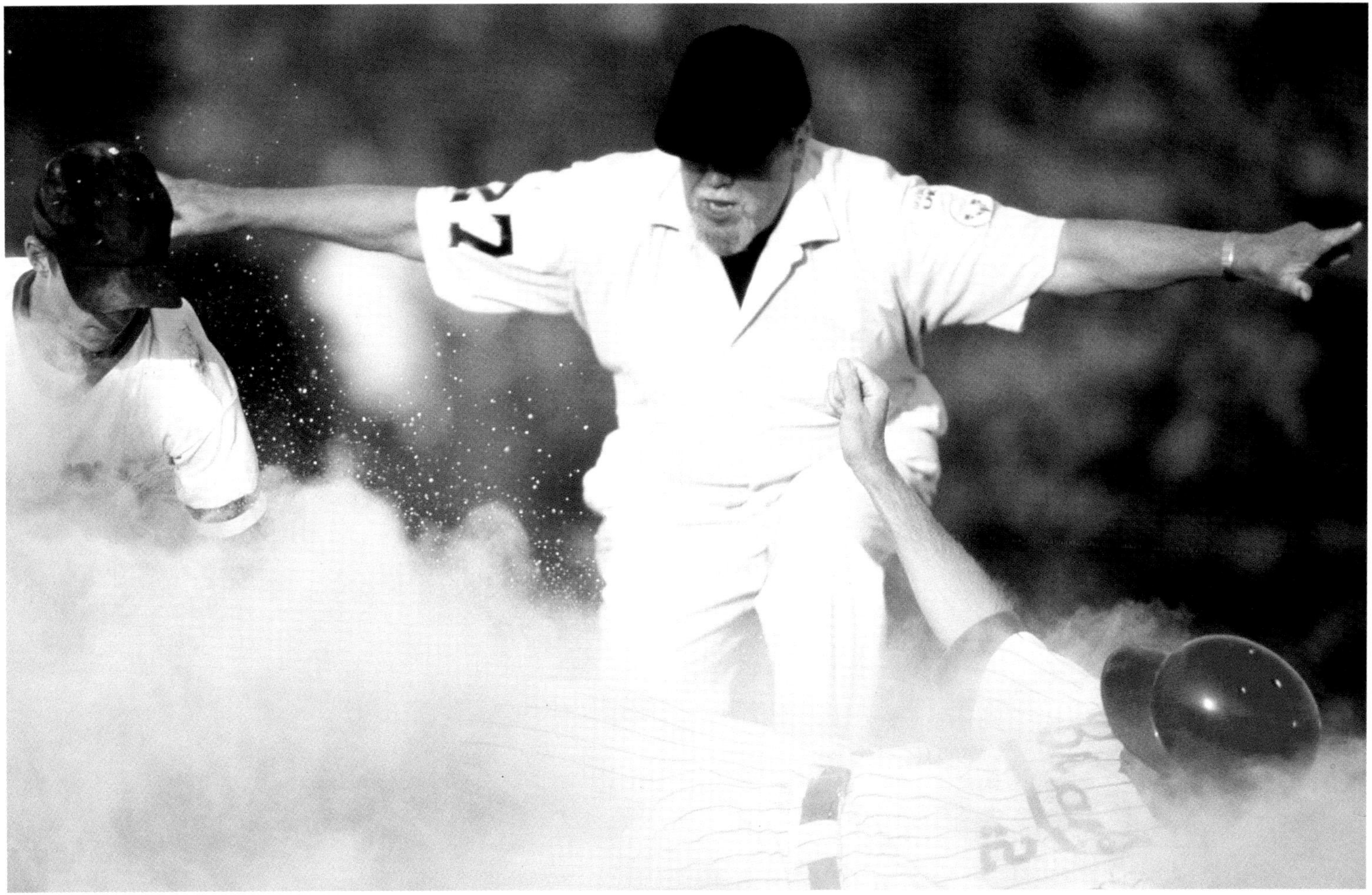

umpire

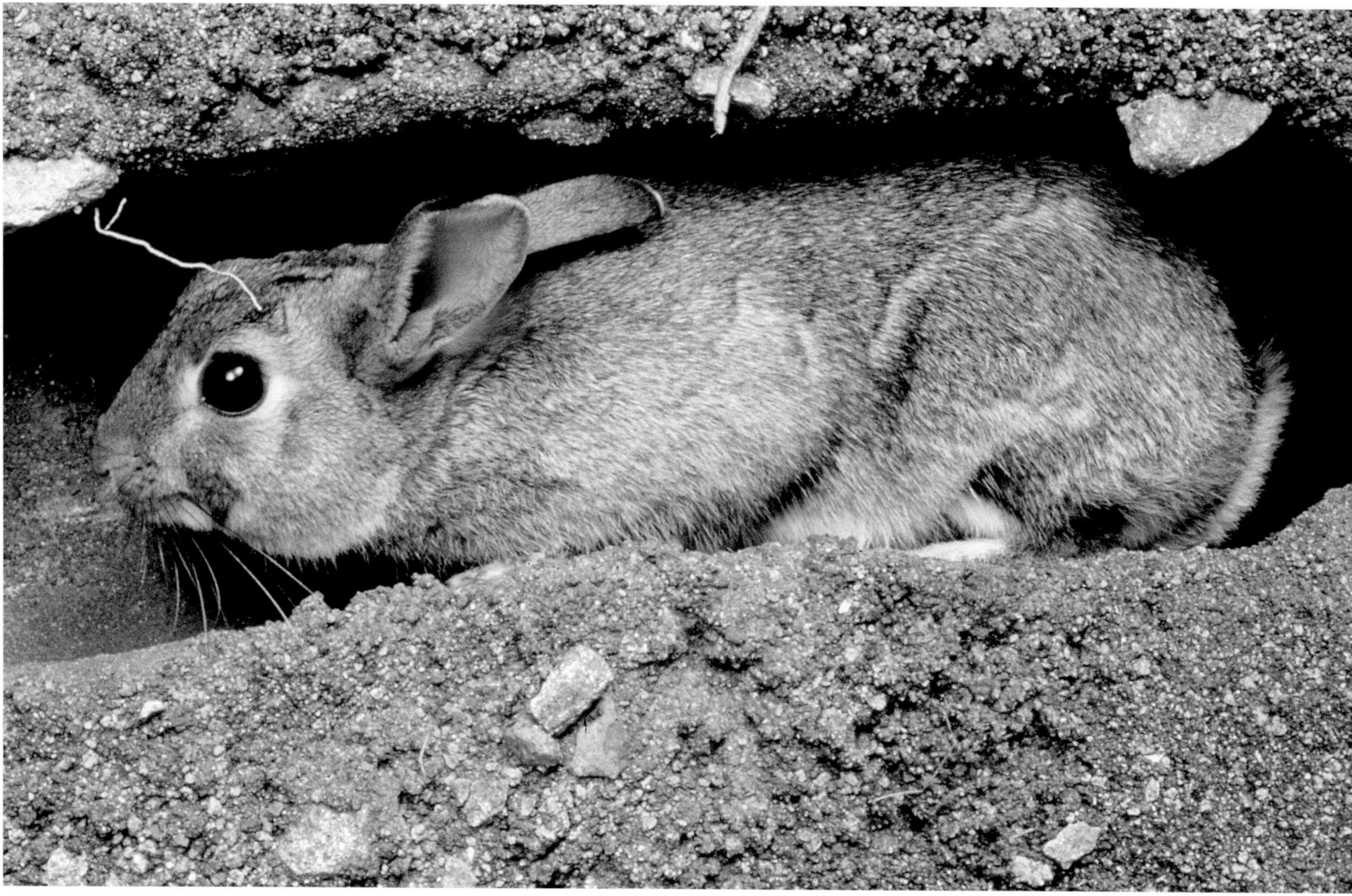

underground

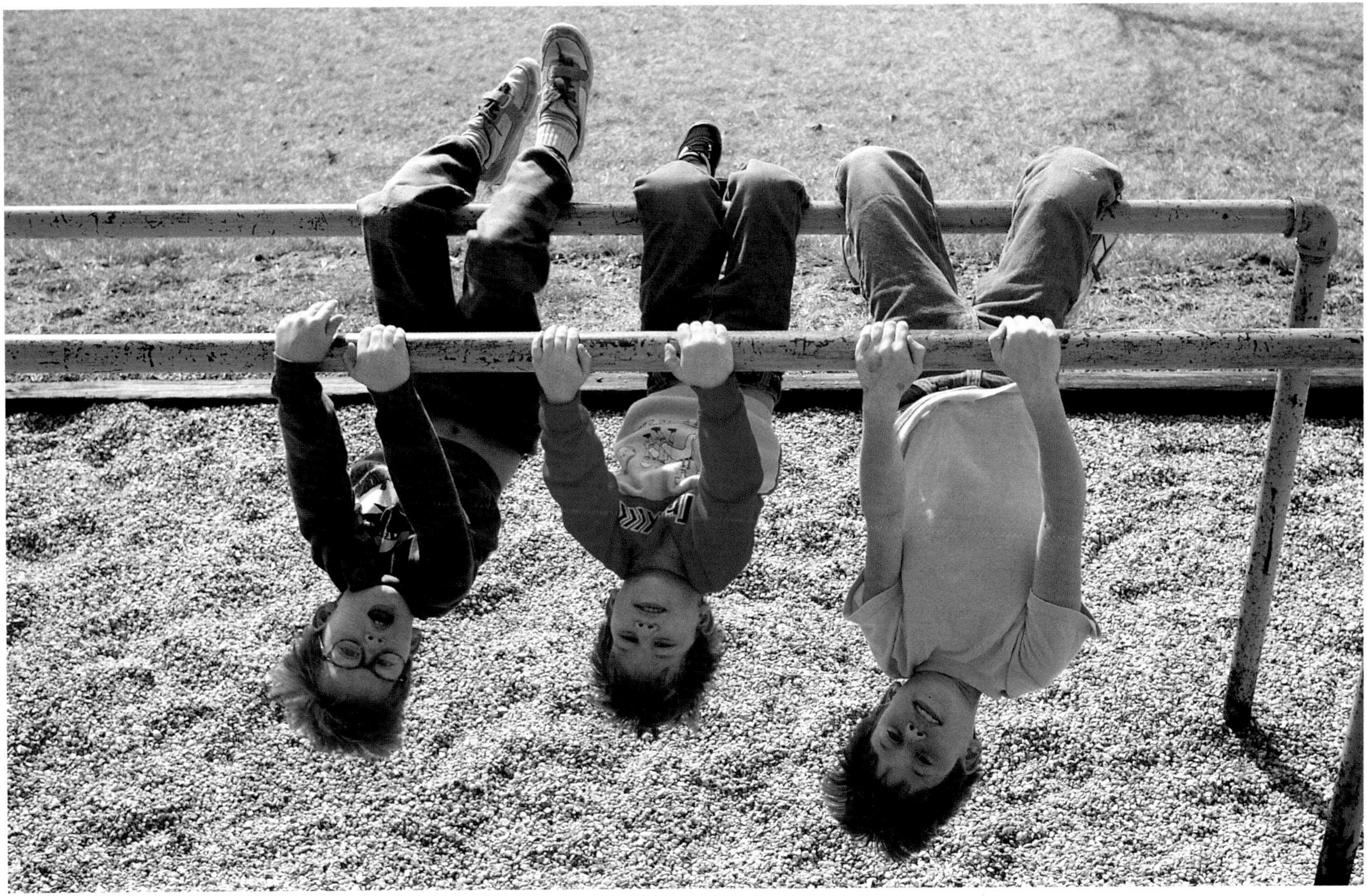

upside-down

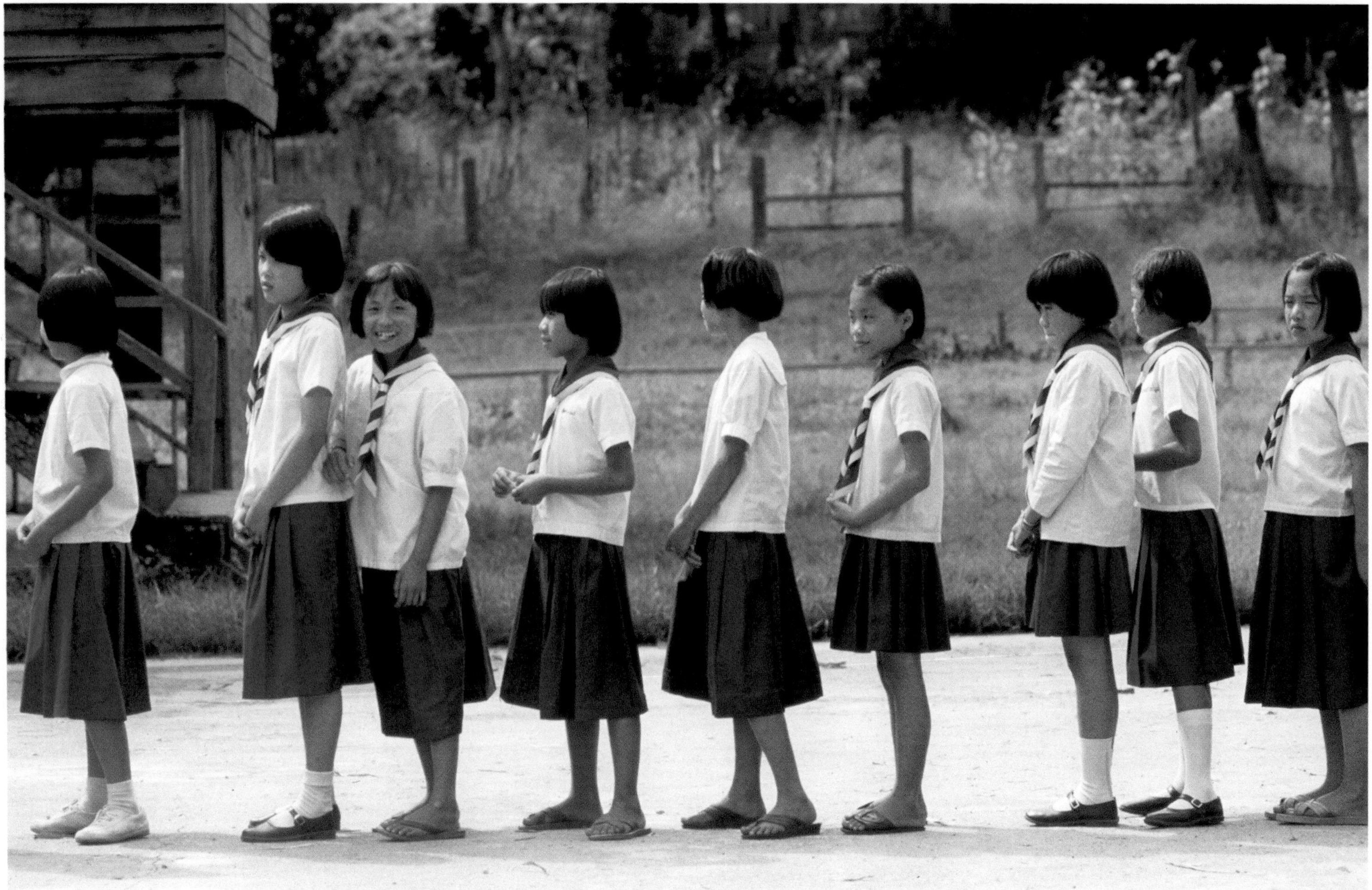

uniform

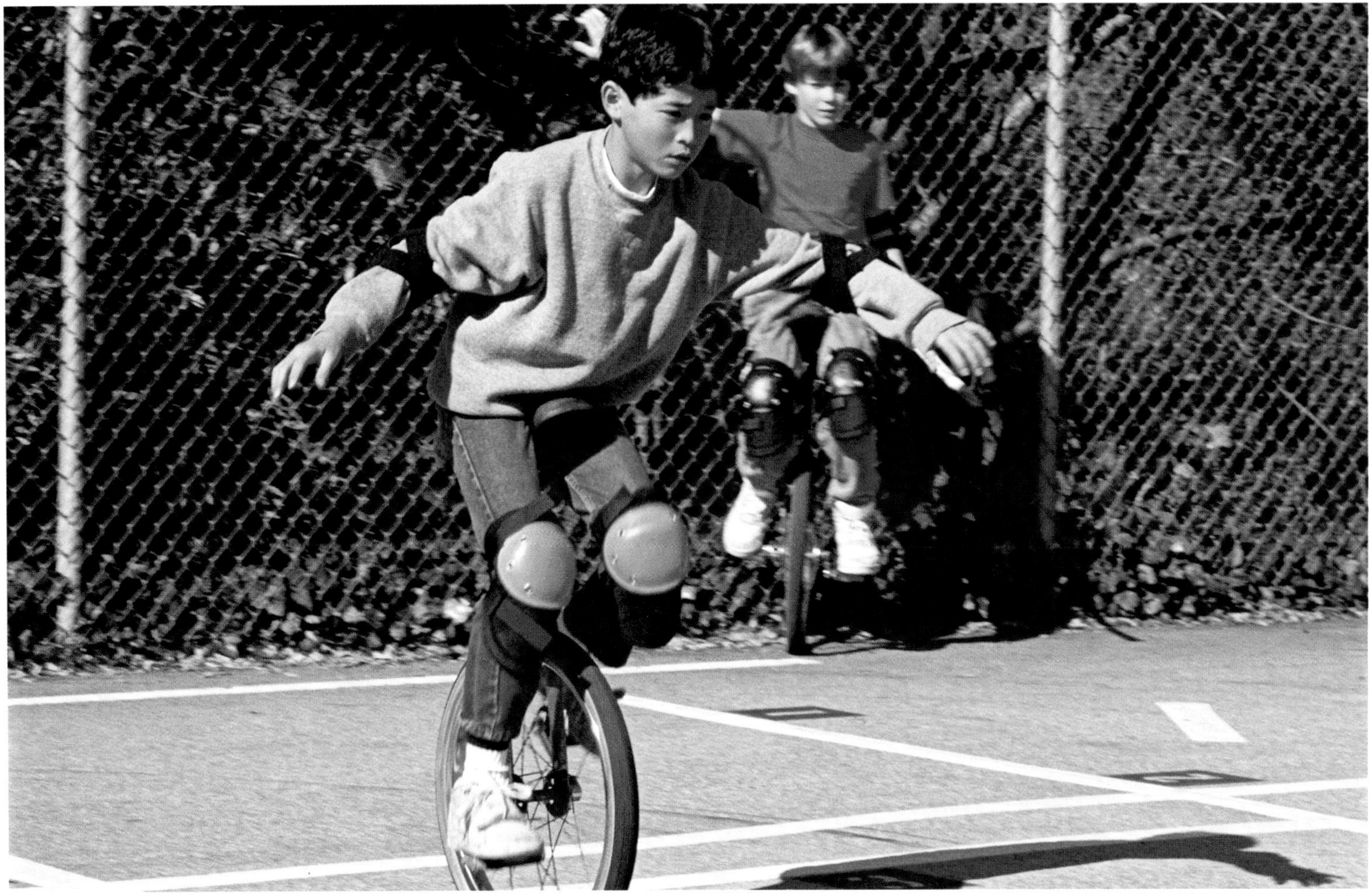

unicycle

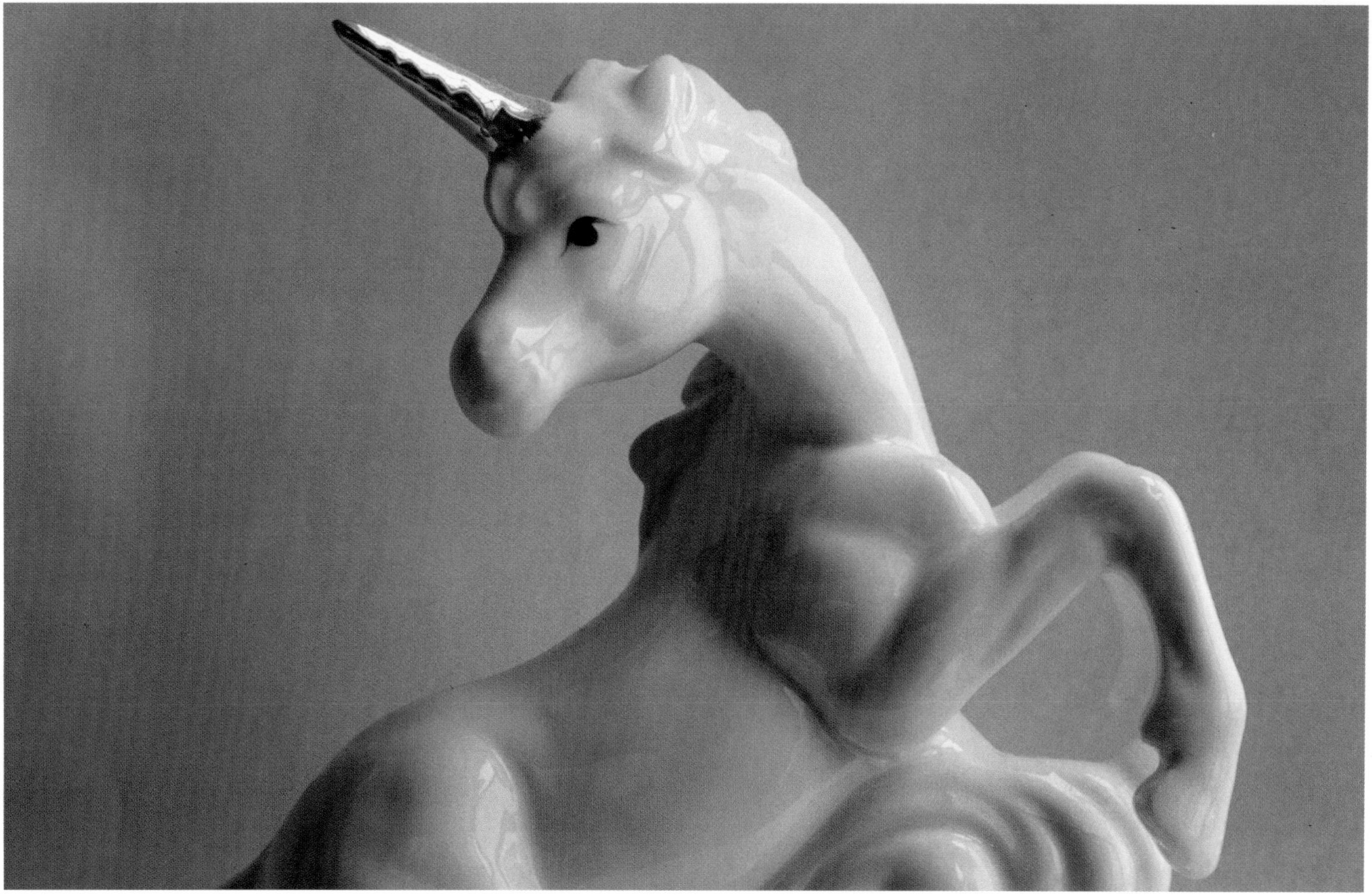

unicorn